CABINET OFFICE

# Future World Trends

*A discussion paper on world trends in population,
resources, pollution etc, and their implications*

LONDON   HER MAJESTY'S STATIONERY OFFICE

ISBN 0 11 630147 3

# Contents

I    Introduction  *1*

II   Population  *2*

III  Food  *5*

IV   Mineral resources  *8*

V    Energy  *11*

VI   Pollution  *13*

VII  Economic aspects  *16*

VIII Modelling  *17*

IX   Conclusions and implications for the United
     Kingdom  *18*

X    Summary  *20*
     Appendix  *25*

# I Introduction

1. Over the past few years the world, and not least the United Kingdom, has witnessed a series of events which may be seen as crises or simply examples of challenges in the developing world scene.

2. Stimulated in part by the Stockholm Conference on the Human Environment and the concurrent public debate, an interdepartmental committee was set up to consider long-term world trends in population, economic growth, resources and environmental effects. In this context, 'long-term' has been taken as referring to time horizons at which the problems which will be encountered cannot be deduced by mere extrapolation from the present. The time-scale varies with subject. For example, for population and energy, concern focuses upon periods well into the next century; for agriculture, interest begins a decade ahead. The main aims of the committee have been to provide critical assessments of information in a field of rapidly growing public interest and to appraise particular key areas to help establish the position to be taken by the United Kingdom in international matters.

3. Public interest in the relation between different aspects of the future scene, population, resources, pollution etc, was stimulated by the publication and discussion of 'Blueprint for Survival' and popular accounts of early mathematical modelling work such as 'World Dynamics' and 'Limits to Growth' by Professor Forrester, Professor Meadows and others working at the Massachusetts Institute of Technology. More recently this interest has been reinforced by the second report to the Club of Rome, 'Mankind at the Turning Point', by Messrs Mesarovic and Pestel. The assumptions, methods and conclusions of some of the earlier studies were discussed exhaustively in particular in two works by the World Bank and by the Science Policy Research Unit at the University of Sussex. Independently, a growing awareness of the increasing interdependence of nations has developed through a number of international gatherings including the World Population Conference in Bucharest (1974), the United Nations (Sixth) Special Session on Raw Materials and Development (1974) and the World Food Conference in Rome (1974).

4. Against this background, the committee has been concerned in the first instance with setting up study capabilities, the Systems Analysis Research Unit (SARU) in the Department of the Environment (DOE), and subsequently with initiating preliminary reviews of the world-wide long-term availability of resources, particularly world food supplies, and the effects of market pressures and pollution control, while always bearing in mind the implications for the United Kingdom. A paper by the then Chief Scientific Adviser (Sir Alan Cottrell), based on its first findings, was published in *Nature* (Vol 245, 12 October 1973). The committee has also critically reviewed much published work on world trends.

5. In the time available the committee has been able to do little more than scratch the surface of the numerous and difficult issues raised. As far as

possible, greatest attention has been paid to those areas where greatest concern has been identified and where adequate data were available. For example, SARU, jointly with the Ministry of Agriculture, Fisheries and Food, the Department of Education and Science and the Ministry of Overseas Development, has been undertaking a study relating estimates of population trends with those of food supplies. On the other hand, the question of mineral resources, where the effort still needed to make an impact both in developing analytical techniques and amassing data is large, has been looked at only relatively briefly.

6. The following paper is presented as a basis for informed discussion of the issues involved. It draws some conclusions from the facts available, given a number of assumptions. Its purpose, however, is not to project or predict the precise position of the world over the next 30 or more years, but rather to analyse present trends and practices and draw out the implications for the future in terms of general trends and likely interactions. The paper does not therefore set out any answers, still less does it define present or future Government policies; it poses a series of questions which merit consideration when Government and governed are seeking to define the future policies for the United Kingdom and their relations to other countries. By its very nature the paper is an interim document. Studies are continuing to extend in breadth and depth knowledge of the trends presented and to identify the rational policy options implied and the implications of nations continuing to pursue existing policies. These studies should also help to ensure that the United Kingdom keeps abreast of similar work in other national and international bodies and, where appropriate, shares resources internationally in the future studies field.

**II Population**
7. Speculative projections of the world's population growth over the next two centuries were prepared by the Population Division of the United Nations Organisation as background material for the World Population Conference, held in Bucharest from 19 to 30 August 1974. These were extrapolations of earlier projections by the United Nations from 1965 to the year 2000. They did not claim to be predictions but were hypothetical figures, derived from assumptions about the paths that declining fertility might follow in eight major areas of the world, leading ultimately to stable levels of population being approached but by different dates in different regions. Bringing about such transitions from high to low fertility rates in the developing world and hence reducing the rate of growth in population implies major changes in their socio-economic structures, as cause and as effect. Even those national Governments in the developing world which are already devoting considerable resources to trying to reduce the levels of fertility focus on the immediate problems of starting on the downward transition rather than on when in the future it might be completed. A more recent and more detailed set of projections from 1970 to 2000 have modified the picture of medium-term world population growth, but nevertheless the earlier long-range projections still serve to show the possible orders of magnitude at which world population numbers might stabilise.

**Fig. 1**

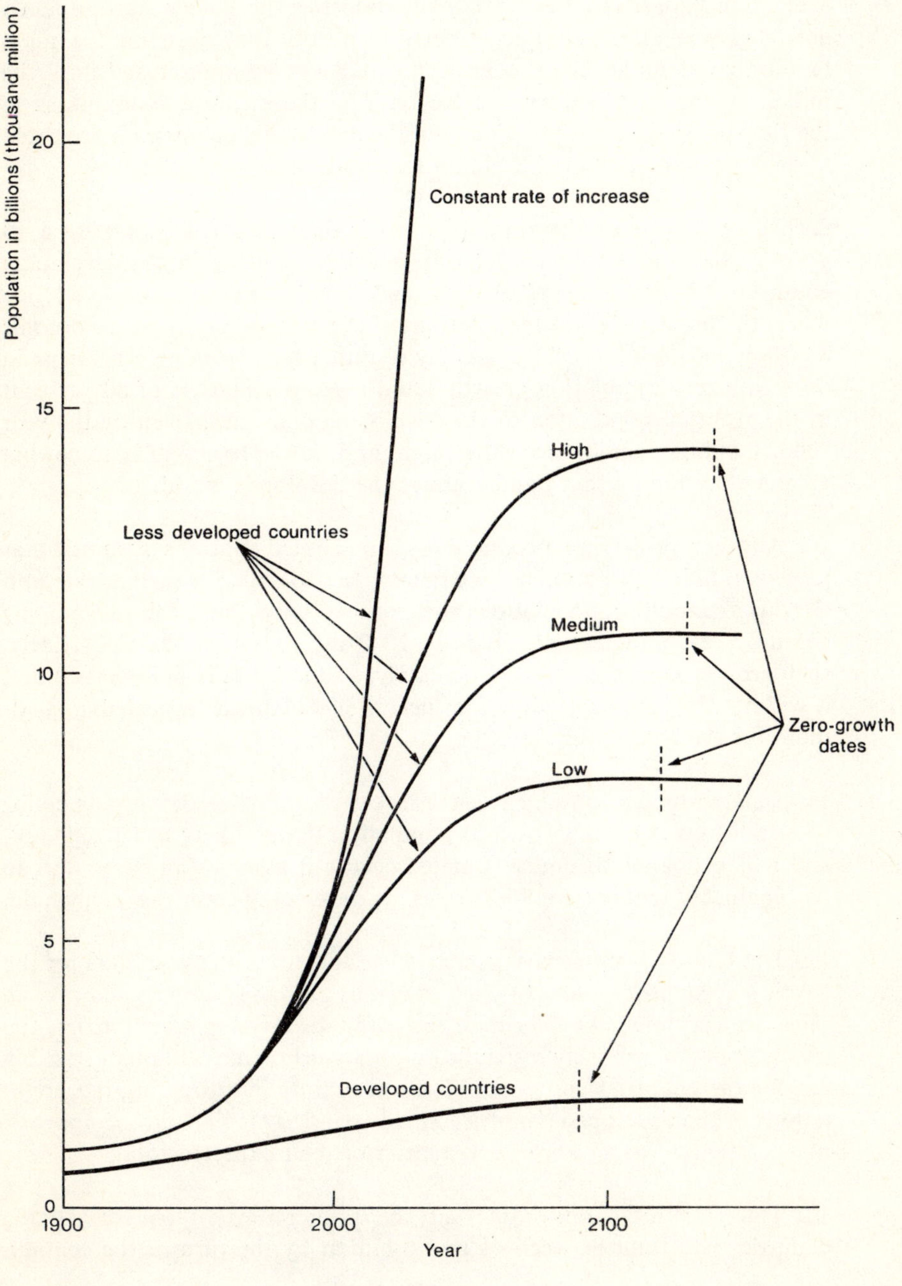

Population in billions (thousand million)

20

15

Constant rate of increase

High

Less developed countries

Medium

10

Zero-growth
dates

Low

5

Developed countries

0

1900          2000          2100

Year

3

8. The United Nations long-range projections are shown in Figure 1. In all cases smooth transitions from the present growth rates to zero growth are assumed. The medium assumptions made in the 1970 projections concerning the rate of decline in fertility levels imply that the populations of the developed countries as a whole may take until the middle of the next century to approach stabilisation in numbers, increasing from the present 1·1 billion to about 1·5 billion. However, population growth rates in the developed world have dropped sharply in recent years and on a current view an ultimate population size of 1·5 billion would be a high rather than a medium figure. For the developing countries the higher starting levels and slower assumed decline in fertility means that even on the most favourable assumptions zero growth would not be approached until the middle of the next century. On the basis of the medium assumptions of the 1965 projections the population of the developing countries is projected to grow from its present 2·8 billion to 10 billion.

9. The sensitivity of these assumptions is demonstrated by taking a 10 years earlier and a 10 years later approach to stability for the developing countries, obtaining so-called 'low' and 'high' variants respectively, for which the projected stable populations of the developing countries become 8 billion and 14 billion. Thus a delay of rather less than one generation in achieving zero population growth could mean an increase of 80 per cent in the eventual population of the developing countries. Even by the year 2000, the difference between the 'high' and 'low' projection is somewhat greater than the present population of the developed world.

10. Another projection produced by the United Nations assumes that present trends will continue indefinitely, the so-called 'constant' variant. On this assumption, populations rise exponentially, that of the developing countries reaching nearly 6 billion by 2000 and 15 billion by 2025. Clearly, such growth cannot continue indefinitely, and indeed the pointers are that it will not, but the projection does nevertheless indicate a probable maximum for the next generation.

11. Demographers consider that the low variant for the developing countries indicates the smallest world population that is likely to be achieved, and it is probably an underestimate because it assumes an early start to the significant reduction in birth rates for developing countries as a whole.

12. The United Nations has produced variants up to the year 2000 for the developed countries in the 1970 series but, as both the numbers and growth rates are very much smaller than those for the developing countries, the effects are comparatively insignificant on a world scale, although possibly not for the countries concerned. The uncertainty in estimating the populations of the developed countries in the year 2100 is likely to be approximately 400 million or about one-quarter of their expected total.

13. Thus the indications are that the populations of the developing countries will total between $4\frac{1}{2}$ and 6 billion by the turn of the century,

and at the very minimum 8 billion and probably 10–15 billion in the long term. One consequence of this is that the population of the developed world, as a percentage of the total world population, is likely to fall from its present value of 30 per cent to around 20 per cent by the year 2000, and possibly to little more than 10 per cent by the end of the next century.

14. Continued rapid population growth in the immediate future is inevitable. Even if fertility rates were to be reduced to replacement level *now*, the existing age structure of the world's population would ensure continuing growth for another two generations. It is this fact which accounts for the long-term sensitivity of total population to stabilisation date.

15. Programmes aimed at reducing the birthrate and promoting small family sizes have met with considerable success in some countries, although in some of the poorest, notably Bangladesh, the overall national response has been disappointing. There are also many Governments, especially in Latin America and Africa, which claim that they need to maintain high rates of population growth in order to develop their maximum national resource potential. However, even these countries accepted the World Population Plan of Action, adopted at the Bucharest Conference, which recognised the right of couples freely and responsibly to determine the number and spacing of their children and to have the information, education and means to do so. The Conference endorsed the view that, in the longer term, voluntary reductions are primarily dependent on changing social attitudes which are more likely to come about as a result of improved living conditions. In any event, the achievement of a smooth and maintained transition to zero population growth will only be brought about by a permanently sustained effort to promote and win acceptance for the goal of small family sizes, and to make available to the populations of the developing countries the services which will allow them to achieve their goals.

## III Food

16. Agricultural production is ultimately limited in two ways:
(a) By natural resources—land, water and raw materials, as well as the energy needed for intensive agricultural production.
(b) By the maldistribution of economic resources, including capital, technology and management, which precludes, in many countries, the achievement of levels of agricultural production which are physically possible.

17. It is estimated that only about one-quarter of the land surface of the world is cultivable. The area currently used for arable farming is probably no more than half of this and the intensity of cultivation varies widely from continuous cropping down to less than one crop annually. Most of the potentially cultivable land is in the tropics; however, in the equatorial forest zone nearly half of such land is at present inaccessible, and much of the remainder is insufficiently fertile to produce food crops economically at present prices.

18. Of all land now cultivated, about 15 per cent is irrigated. The amount of land which could be irrigated by natural fresh water (either from wells or by storage and distribution from rivers) is not known precisely but is probably at least double the existing area. Much of this potential is in developing countries in the tropics. Nonetheless, only a relatively small proportion of the total area could be served by freshwater sources within a range which can be foreseen as possibly becoming economically viable. All of these areas could in theory be irrigated by desalination of sea water, although in most cases transport over long distances would be necessary. However, the present cost in money and energy terms of desalination is generally so high as to preclude serious consideration, other than on a strictly local scale such as that of small wealthy islands, and this situation is not expected to alter in the foreseeable future.

19. There is new land to be cleared in Africa and in South America, but by and large the more fertile areas with reliable rainfall have already been used; and a further problem is the spread of unskilful subsistence agriculture into lands of marginal rainfall or fertility. The rate of increase in yields of crops in the developing countries could be improved substantially; modern technology is as yet applied to only a small proportion of the area. In short, there is scope for major increases in world food production to meet the needs of a rising population by increasing the yield of the land already farmed.

20. In terms of purely physical factors it is theoretically possible to meet the food needs of the estimated population of the world for the next 30 to 40 years, without resort to unconventional agricultural techniques, assuming the highest United Nations population projection, and allowing for 25 per cent wastage (the current estimate) in production, storage, processing and distribution. Provided that global food requirements are met by an extension of food consumption according to existing dietary patterns, rather than, say, a general shift towards those of the developed world, it is likely that overall protein supplies will also be adequate. But it must be emphasised that these statements take no account of the enormous economic, social and political problems involved in increasing food production to these levels. There are problems of providing the developing countries with the necessary capital for investment. Development aid for agriculture at present amounts to only 0·1 per cent of national incomes of developed nations: there is international agreement that more aid must be directed towards rural development and food production, but progress in achieving this will be influenced by many factors, including the long lead times involved in working up new projects and the shortage of qualified technical and managerial staff in many countries. Some stimulus may come from rising market prices, making agricultural investment competitive with alternative commercial opportunities, and international agencies may help in promoting viable schemes by pre-investment studies, by contributions to costs and by the loan of skilled specialists. But these alone will not ensure the transfer of resources to developing countries on the scale required.

21. Much of the tropical zone with the greatest potential for land development is sparsely populated and far from the main centres of food consumption. Massive migration of labour, as well as capital, would be needed, and high costs of distribution have also to be met. Moreover, if the world is to be adequately fed, consumers' income must be adequate. To the extent that these problems preclude the optimum development of the areas with greatest potential, the financial and energy costs of achieving equivalent output in less favourable areas will be that much greater.

22. Continued increase of food production in developing countries depends on increasing supplies of energy, notably for the provision of fertilisers and water, against a background of rising energy costs and competition from other energy uses. The balance between food production and the size of the effective world demand for food will depend not only on population increase but also on the rates of economic growth. Increasing costs per unit output of fertilisers will almost inevitably lead to a slowing down in the increase in food production in developing countries. This, coupled with a rising population, could mean the virtual disappearance in the future of food surpluses, which are necessary to mitigate the effects of droughts and other crop failures. If the developed countries are to refrain from pre-empting any food surpluses available, they will need to consider the provision of greater storage facilities to insure against fluctuations in world supply, bearing in mind the enormous capital expenditure which would be involved.

23. The theoretical food level described up to 2010 (paragraphs 17–20) is therefore unlikely to be reached in practice because:
(a) There are likely to be continuing economic, social and political barriers to the optimal policy of concentrating the expansion of output in the tropics.
(b) Similar obstacles are likely to restrict the equitable global distribution of the food provided.
(c) There is likely to be continuing growth in the consumption of animal protein foods among the richer communities, and the conversion of crops to animal proteins is very inefficient.
(d) The possibility of major disasters such as widespread crop disease epidemics or severe drought occurring simultaneously in the primary grain producing areas cannot be dismissed. The possible effects of long-term climatological changes are now being seriously considered in this context, although current evidence that such changes will occur in the foreseeable future is not convincing.
(e) The rising cost of obtaining sharply increased quantities of fertilisers and pesticides at much higher prices will raise serious problems. By contrast, while pollution dangers could place limits on the use of certain pesticides, problems are unlikely to be caused by pesticides in general provided they are kept under control.

24. Fisheries are unlikely to supply a large element of the world's food needs but they will continue to play a significant part in the provision of

essential animal protein, particularly in specific locations. Although about half the world's total sustainable yield of conventional marine fish and shellfish species is now being caught, the sea is capable of yielding also very substantial quantities of unconventional species (species that are either not now caught or are discarded for lack of acceptable economics, technologies, or markets) which offer opportunities for the development of unconventional protein foods and of synthetic animal feed (which could be particularly important to the United Kingdom in reducing its dependence on expensive imports). Further, there is scope for the development of marine fish farming, and in the more distant future on substantial manipulation of the aquatic environment.

25. In the century beyond 2010, if population stabilisation has not been substantially achieved, the physical constraints imposed by land and water availability and rising energy requirements will become much more severe: but before that, in the absence of a massive transfer of resources to the developing countries, world population growth or health is much more likely to be rigorously limited by countries' domestic food production.

26. The most urgent issue is that of the priority now given by developing countries to their own food supplies *per capita*. This involves concern with both the rate of population growth and of agricultural development. Greatly increased international effort will be essential even for the maintenance of the present precarious balance between food and population. Failure can only result in a limitation of population growth by higher death rates. Both increased economic resources and concentration on the essential priorities of food and population are needed to achieve stability; otherwise our maximum foreseeable efforts in food production will only buy time without resolving the problem. More scientific resources need to be devoted to developing acceptable methods of contraception, so that as social attitudes change with improving economic development, the benefits of increasing agricultural output will no longer be eliminated by too rapid a growth of population.

### IV Mineral resources

27. Some natural resources such as food and timber are continuously renewable whereas others such as fossil fuels and metalliferous ores are depleted continuously. However, the simplistic approach that 'known reserves' will be used up in so many years on current trends can be seriously misleading. It involves the tacit assumption that there is a 'given' amount of resources waiting to be used, and that when these have been consumed we must revert to a subsistence economy. Only in the most absolute sense is this true.

28. A mechanism operates as follows to bring supply and demand for mineral resources into equilibrium:
(a) Continuing demand for a mineral depletes known resources.
(b) Scarcity of mineral raises prices and profits.
(c) Profits are invested in geological surveys to find further supplies of ore at a lower grade or further high grade ores in more remote places.

(d) Higher prices for mineral raise manufacturers' costs.

(e) High prices encourage producers to apply improved technology.

(f) Higher costs stimulate research into substitute materials.

(g) Supply and demand come into equilibrium at a new price level.

The mechanism has worked very well in the past. Records show that the average real price of many minerals has remained almost constant for over 80 years. A series of technological advances in mining, metallurgy and geophysics until recently also compensated to some extent for declining grades and increased inaccessibility. However, these advantages have been offset by the substantial scale of finance now required for a modern mining venture.

29. On the demand side increased sophistication in the use of materials has provided substitutes for many traditional raw materials so that expected shortages have failed to materialise, although it should not be assumed that because substitution mechanisms have operated smoothly in the past they can always be depended upon in the future. There are some inputs (e.g. energy, phosphates) which have literally no substitutes and efforts to find alternative supplies of other resources could lead to such catastrophic side-effects that there may be no alternative to doing without them.

30. Smooth replacement of one material by another requires adequate investment in the substitute well in advance, and current consumption must be sacrificed so that appropriate investment in the substitute can be made. A long lead time before a project becomes profitable implies a low discount rate and a distant time horizon. Because mining companies consider that their operations are inherently risky they usually apply a discount rate higher than that used in manufacturing industry. Companies pursuing a rational exploration policy very seldom invest in geological surveys to establish reserves of much greater than 20 years. This may account for the relatively low figures for reserves published by them.

31. From the viewpoint of depletion, minerals fall into two categories, depending on their relative abundance in the crust and their mode of occurrence.

(a) *Virtually inexhaustible minerals*

The Earth's crust contains large quantities of aluminium (8 per cent), calcium (5·1 per cent), iron (5·8 per cent), sodium and potassium (4 per cent), magnesium (2·8 per cent) and titanium (0·86 per cent), and it seems hardly credible that more than an insignificant fraction of those minerals will ever be incorporated into human artifacts. Aluminium, iron and magnesium are already important industrial metals; the applications of titanium are increasing and even sodium has potentialities as a conductor. Many metals are used for traditional reasons; not because they are ideal or abundant but because it was easy to separate them from their ores by primitive pyrometallurgical techniques.

(b) *Potentially exhaustible minerals*

Most of the other metallic elements in the crust occur at much lower concentrations than those referred to in (a) above, and most of these metals could be replaced by others which are more abundant. However, several of the metals have special properties that are very useful and could only be replaced with great difficulty and expense. If depletion of these minerals was occurring one might expect to see a gradual increase in the cost of production and price. However, an examination of the time series data suggests that when the effects of the trade cycle are smoothed out and allowance is made for inflation the overall change in the price level is quite small. Similarly investigations into the cost in terms of labour and capital of mining and refining have shown a consistent downward trend. On the other hand, average grade of ore mined has been falling consistently, suggesting that the high grade material is becoming exhausted and forcing operators to concentrate on large low-grade ore bodies. The apparent contradiction can be reconciled if one recalls the rapid advance in the technology of mining and mineral separation, and the large energy component in mining operations which has until recently had a downward trend in real terms. This process cannot, however, go on for ever. It has already been counteracted by the substantial increase in capital now required to develop a mine. Greater energy intensity will also, in due course, lead to higher costs.

32. The recycling of scrap materials will continue to play an important role in the supply of minerals to industry. In the United Kingdom, at present, non-ferrous metal requirements obtained from recycled scrap range from 26 per cent for aluminium to 62 per cent for lead. However, recycling has several important limitations. Some uses of metal (e.g. zinc in galvanising, lead in anti-knock compounds) are inherently dispersive and recovery is practically impossible. The cost of recycling, either in economic terms or in resource usage, may be higher than the cost of primary metal (e.g. scrap iron contaminated with other metals). Current scrap availability is a function of consumption at the time when the equipment was produced. In a growth situation the supply of scrap from obsolete equipment will always lag behind the demand even though the rates of growth may be the same. The point at which these factors have a serious effect on demand for the primary raw material depends upon the relative economics of the processes. In a world context, recycling in the developed countries might make a significant contribution to the life of supplies of certain metals, although the problems of collecting and sorting can be formidable.

33. There are thus no hard and fast physical limits to resources; the limits are economic and technological and can vary widely. The materials needed are available and will continue to be if the cost in capital, labour and energy are met. Resources are in fact a function of costs; as lower grade ores are consumed the necessary allocation of resources to the mineral and energy sectors must increase. This diversion of resources means that there are less goods available for consumption but does not necessarily entail a persistent depression of standards of living. Absolute shortages of minerals are not likely to appear as insuperable difficulties in the period under review. However, national questions of environment and security of

supplies and international constraints will undoubtedly affect the availability of raw materials and the manner in which they are utilised.

34. Though these conclusions suggest a qualified optimism they do not, of course, mean that work should not be undertaken to identify those minerals for which particular difficulties may occur both in the short and long term. Work to this end is in hand. In order to investigate the value of modelling in the mineral resources area, a study has been carried out by the Programmes Analysis Unit, Harwell. A model was constructed of the supply, use and recycling of lead on a global scale covering a period up to 100 years from now. It was concluded that although this was of sufficient versatility and credibility to be of value as a long-term behavioural probe of materials consumption, it could not at present provide a basis for policy decisions. For that, the technique would need refining and further assessment in a broader context; at present it is doubtful whether adequate input data could be obtained at reasonable cost. Mineral availability is nevertheless a matter of vital importance for the United Kingdom economy so that any potentially useful policy tools must be explored. The work is therefore being kept under review, in order to assess the use that could be made of such techniques in analysing policy options in respect of future changes in the relative scarcities of different materials, and so point to profitable directions for research.

**V Energy**
35. Energy in its various forms is one of the most critical needs of mankind, but in the forms in which it is presently used, i.e. principally through the transformation of fossil fuels to useful heat, expectations of the life of future supplies are necessarily finite. However, electric power derived from nuclear fission has shown relatively rapid growth in meeting part of the energy demand: for example, in OECD countries it is expected, according to the latest published estimates, to contribute about 6–7 per cent to total energy supplies in 1980 and perhaps 10–13 per cent in 1985. The table at Appendix 1 illustrates the drastic effect of exponential growth of demand on energy reserves. Long before exhaustion, however, fossil fuel supply would in practice be severely curtailed in an attempt to maintain a reserves-to-production ratio of around 10. However, given the successful full-scale development of the breeder reactor, uranium supplies should last as far into the future as can be seen. Unconventional sources of energy, e.g. geothermal, solar, wind, waves, tides and controlled nuclear fusion, are all under world-wide examination, while working examples, on a relatively small scale, exist of harnessed wind, geothermal and tidal power. These methods draw upon primary sources which are either regularly self-renewing or virtually inexhaustible. However, their widespread use lies far into the future, and even then will rest on their ability to satisfy the economic and environmental criteria which are in force at the time.

36. The period considered here does not extend into the distant future when novel energy sources become dominant, and for which it is possible only to speculate about availability and cost. Instead, it concentrates on

the period between the apparently plentiful fuel of the 1960s and the time when the supply of some fossil fuels begins to taper off and the human race becomes increasingly dependent on finding at least one plentiful, workable and not too costly alternative. A basic problem is to identify the most likely combination of the many different ways modern society can adjust itself to high cost and potentially insecure and scarce energy supplies. Energy is not the only or even the most scarce and vulnerable resource needed by man, but technically it is possible to ameliorate the effects of shortages in other resources provided sufficient energy is available. The extent and form of the response will vary in different countries and regions of the world, but the general orientation of new energy developments will follow the normal laws of supply and demand provided these are allowed to operate freely.

37. Summaries of published fuel reserves are shown in Appendix 1, but, because of the general uncertainty of the world energy situation, these figures can only be taken as an illustration of the relative magnitudes of the various resources and of the stark consequences of sustained exponential growth of energy demand. Historic growth rates have fluctuated but the average has been around 5 per cent. Higher fuel prices will tend to reduce these and increase the number, extent and recoverability of economically exploitable deposits. The future rate of economic growth is, however, likely to be the chief determining factor of the level of fuel consumption.

38. Energy problems are providing a strong inducement to international co-operation. For example, both the International Energy Agency and the European Economic Community (EEC) are considering to what extent market forces may need to be reinforced to stimulate energy conservation projects and the development of alternative sources of energy, and how this can best be done. They are also determining energy research and development priorities.

39. The future divides into two broad time horizons. In the short and medium term there will continue to be no physical shortage of fossil fuels, though the unequal distribution of resources creates problems and has led to high prices. In the longer term, fossil fuels (particularly oil and gas) will become increasingly scarce. The timing of this development is very uncertain but it could, on the basis of what is now known about reserves and recovery rates, be beginning to take place before the turn of the century. The smoothness with which the world economy adjusts to an increasing scarcity of fossil fuels will depend, given the long lead times involved, on the early and successful development of the new technologies required and on their timely introduction on a scale sufficient to have a significant effect on the world situation. Massive research and development programmes have been launched, particularly in the United States of America, to increase the availability of indigenous fuel and energy resources, including solar, geothermal and, on a smaller scale, wind power. The proposed ERDA (Energy Research and Development Administration)

budget for 1976 is over $4,000 million, over 60 per cent being for nuclear. Energy saving campaigns have been launched throughout the developed world and increased technical and research effort is being devoted to energy conservation. Energy conservation measures are an important aid to achieving a balance of supply and demand, and can make a worthwhile if limited contribution to delaying the exhaustion of fuel reserves. It is to be hoped that, in response to higher energy prices, publicity and exhortations, energy conservation may become a desirable social habit, in the same way as hygiene and cleanliness have become an integral part of modern life. However, high energy prices could also have socially detrimental effects, for example by retarding economic progress in developing countries, and possibly leading to hardship among the lower income groups in the more developed countries.

40. Beyond the mid-1980s there are prospects that the fruits of research and development and particularly the expansion of nuclear power will curtail the scope for unrestricted monopolistic exploitation of scarce resources. Indeed, if nuclear fission power should take over as the main energy growth component, the need for large-scale development of other non-nuclear alternatives to depletable fossil fuels may become limited to such specialised fields as transport fuels. There are some unresolved technological problems, but the scale of world-wide commitment to the thermal reactor, and the pressure for successful development of fast breeder reactors with high fuel efficiency, is so large that there is hope that resources will be found to overcome current or future obstacles.

41. The massive capital investment required for future energy production could, of course, lead to severe economic problems, not exclusively confined to the developing countries. However, the prospect of self-sufficiency in coal, oil and gas in the next decade, lasting possibly into the 1990s or even beyond, should imply that for a long period ahead availability of energy will not be a constraint on the growth of the gross national product (GNP) of the United Kingdom, in spite of the problems in the immediate future. If the gross national product continues to grow steadily, resources should become available to meet expected energy demands.

## VI Pollution
42. Pollution has become an increasing national and international concern in the last two decades. Most incidents which have served to focus this concern have been due to localised concentrations of particular pollutants and, although the number of incidents has increased, widespread adverse effects due to pollution in Britain have declined. There is no conclusive evidence of damage to human health or ecological stability on a global scale due to a universally distributed pollutant (except that the consequences of the fallout from nuclear explosions have led to statistical predictions of increased damage to living resources, although there has to date been no medical evidence that this damage has occurred). The most quoted examples of global trends in pollution—for example, the gradual increase in the proportion of carbon dioxide in the atmosphere, chlorofluoro-

13

carbons in the stratosphere, and the trace quantities of DDT and other pesticides to be found in oceans and wild life throughout the world—are no more than changes in pollutant level without, as yet, proven long-term global consequences for living 'targets'. However, it remains necessary to be watchful lest increased pollutant levels in the environment should have unwelcome effects, either through the creation of more local 'hot spots' or through the elevation of the general level of contamination of ocean and atmosphere to the point at which there are undesirable climatic or ecological changes.

43. Many of the most noxious substances are now being released in diminishing amounts and their concentration in the biosphere, at least in the United Kingdom, is falling. This is because of recognition of the need for abatement and the development and use of increasingly efficient pollution control technology. However, the concentrations of, in particular, persistent pollutants need watching since at certain levels they may present problems; and the significance attached to particular pollutants may change in the light of further information or further research. Recent international agreements ought to lead to a progressive reduction in dumping and in the discharge of noxious substances and other potential pollutants into the sea, and their levels in the ocean and in marine life, insofar as these are due to man's activities, should begin to fall.

44. It is impracticable to list all major pollutants and impossible to predict their future levels which will depend on the rate and character of future development. However, except for sulphur oxides, a continuing decline is forecast in industrial emissions such as acidic and alkaline vapours, particulates and heavy metals and in persistent organohalogens such as DDT, for which substitutes either exist or are being sought. Except for carbon dioxide, a slowing down in the upward trend of emission of pollutants from motor vehicles is likely, since most developed countries are adopting standards that will halt, or even reverse, this trend within their borders. However any reduction in pollution from vehicles beyond that already planned may involve penalties of increased energy usage which might not be acceptable. In the United Kingdom, as in other industrial countries, the volume per capita of solid waste of all kinds increases with the material standard of living, and the volume of effluent returning to our rivers after treatment also rises considerably.

45. Increased use of nuclear rather than fossil fuel will also limit the emission of carbon dioxide, sulphur oxides and particulates, although it will inevitably generate increased quantities of radioactive waste, posing increased management and disposal problems. These problems are being closely examined; and they might in the long term be lessened by the development of some of the alternative energy sources mentioned in paragraph 35 above. Meanwhile, since the oceans have an enormous but not unlimited capacity to receive and dilute radioactive wastes, countries with nuclear power programmes must ensure that this capacity is not restricted unnecessarily but is used intelligently.

46. The disposal of heat from power stations is one of many important considerations taken into account in their design and siting. The anticipated increase in energy generation in coming decades may lead to an increasing problem in this regard. In Britain, with her long coastline, where large volumes of water are available for cooling, this problem is likely to be less acute than elsewhere, although significant environmental and amenity considerations will need to be taken into account in every siting decision. More of a regional problem may arise in areas such as Central Western Europe where waste heat cannot be so readily discharged to water. It has been suggested that the discharge of this heat to the atmosphere might eventually have a significant climatic effect. Longer term and more widespread changes in the temperature of air and water cannot be discounted but these, and any consequent global climatic changes, appear likely to be small when compared with naturally occurring long term climatic fluctuations. It is too early to say whether global thermal effects could ultimately become significant, although the possibility must continually be borne in mind. Unlike some other pollutants, all surplus heat must ultimately reach the environment. The greater use of waste heat, for say district heating, will however reduce overall heat pollution if, as a result, fuel is saved. Increased reliance on energy sources (such as solar, tidal, wind etc) which, overall, add no energy to the environment will further reduce total heat pollution.

47. Pollutants will continue to be an inevitable accompaniment of man's increasingly technological activity, and there will always be wastes to dispose of in the environment. Such disposal is a legitimate procedure provided the finite capacity of the environment to disperse and degrade them is not over-taxed. Within this absolute limitation the extent to which society will allow the environment to be used depends on several factors, the most important being man's assessment of the condition of the environment and his will and ability to exercise control over emissions. Decisions on the application of this control are governed by the costs and benefits of the activity that leads to the generation of pollution; the nature and cost of the damage (both direct and indirect) caused by the pollutants; the value society places on creating or maintaining a certain quality of environment; and the effectiveness and cost of various control measures. In the future as research across a broad front and the developing overall scheme for monitoring and assessment leads to better understanding of the vulnerability of 'targets' (including ecological systems as well as man and animals) and the levels of pollutant likely to affect them; as the testing of new substances for environmental impacts becomes increasingly more effective, and as the capacity to control emissions of polluting substances (or to substitute less polluting substances for them) improves, it is to be expected that the frequency with which pollution will be allowed to reach levels at which measurable damage may begin will decrease. Problems may however continue to be met where exposure leads to effects that do not become apparent for a considerable time or where apparently acceptable procedures lead to the slow build up of pollutant levels over a period. Our ability to become aware of such effects will in part depend on the sophisti-

cation and predictive ability of the monitoring and assessment systems developed. But unexpected developments are always possible, given the increasing range and sophistication of substances in use; and accidents (or the failure of control measures due to other causes such as social or economic disruption or strife) will always remain a hazard of greater or lesser significance depending on the nature of the substances involved.

48. The projection in the previous paragraph is based on experience and is essentially optimistic. In most developed countries pollution has become a diminishing problem as awareness, scientific understanding and technological capabilities have grown; in Europe, the EEC has embarked on the implementation of a wide-ranging environment programme. The Organisation for Economic Co-operation and Development has collected estimates of the expenditure on the control of environmental pollution in member countries. These are usually less than 2 per cent of GNP but estimates are subject to a wide margin of error because of the difficulty of defining the attributable costs. There can be wide variations from country to country in the cost of preserving a given environmental quality. There is a tendency, however, for the energy cost of pollution abatement or prevention to rise disproportionately as populations grow and the standard of living and technological development increase. Wealthier societies tend to demand increasingly higher environmental standards and if these are to be achieved at an acceptable cost, increasing effort needs to be devoted to the development of better and safer technologies. However, the developing countries may find it difficult, as they go through the early stages of industrialisation, to meet the pollution standards adopted by developed countries.

## VII Economic aspects

49. Having considered the likely trends in population growth and essential resources it is important to assess the ability of the market to continue to allocate resources and to identify options for a governmental response to market failure. In theoretical and qualitative terms good progress in economic analysis of resource allocation has been made over the years, and this type of analysis is increasingly applied to specific problems. The most common criterion for evaluating the allocation of resources is the 'maximisation of welfare' and the price mechanism will, in general, achieve this result, subject to the distribution of income and wealth being socially and politically acceptable. However, evidence to the contrary should be pursued by a careful study to reveal the nature of the market failure. Government intervention may then be necessary. The causes of market failure include—inferior information; time-lags in response to price changes; absence of competition; existence of a discrepancy between private and social discount rates; lack of ownership by some person or institution (for example, fishing in international waters: there is no incentive for individuals to reduce catches by observing a closed season or by restricting net gauges, even though to do so would benefit the community as a whole); differences between private and social attitudes towards risk taking; and the existence of external factors generally (that is the existence

of a gap between the costs and benefits of some course of action as seen by the body responsible for taking decisions, and the costs and benefits seen by the community as a whole). Research may be needed to identify other market imperfections.

50. It is also recognised that Government may be increasingly faced with situations in which it has to intervene to ensure supplies of vital materials, or to develop substitutes. There is, however, no general prescription for Government action in all individual cases and rigorous examination of the market situation in each case should, therefore, be carried out before intervention is considered. Consequently, it is important to have as much relevant information as possible in Government, and, subject to overriding considerations such as national security, to encourage the wide dissemination and exchange of such information.

51. Economic analysis of resource allocation can contribute to firm policy decisions, but accurate formal solution to many problems may never be possible, despite the expectation that forecasting techniques will improve with time. Research work is continuing across a broad front and there is no obvious individual bottleneck, the removal of which would permit a substantial improvement in analytical capability. On the other hand it may be necessary to bring about a shift in the balance of economic research in favour of applied economics and of the faster development and improvement of the basic sources of data which are essential to both Government and the market.

## VIII Modelling

52. A mathematical model is basically an ordered set of equations describing the relationships between discrete parts of a complex system. Such models may have an important part to play in the study of future world trends, not only in the separate fields mentioned in the report but also in investigations into the inter-relationships between them. The technique of computer modelling has been widely used in recent decades to study problems in both the physical and social sciences and is most frequently applied to systems which are inherently so complicated that they cannot easily be examined by conventional mathematical methods. A particular advantage of the technique is that it is possible by simulation to study the results of changes in the numerical relationship between different variables.

53. The original world dynamic models produced by Professors Forrester and Meadows at the Massachusetts Institute of Technology (MIT) were deficient, not only in their data base but also in the over-emphasis on physical aspects of the problem and their high degree of aggregation. Since their publication, the MIT models have been examined by groups throughout the world and attempts made to improve on them. It is likely to be beyond the scope of any one group—or even country—to provide results quickly, comprehensively and reliably, especially as the early work has pointed to the importance of a thoroughly scientific and objective approach. Fortunately, this is a field in which the work of different groups can contribute effectively to overall progress.

54. The preliminary findings of the principal research groups indicate a consensus view emerging on the base data and on the most effective forms of model structure. The broad conclusions of the separate studies are not dissimilar and place much less stress on global physical limitations than on the problems of distribution.

55. The Systems Analysis Research Unit in the Department of the Environment has made extensive feasibility tests on alternative model structures. These indicate that it is possible to overcome the principal defects and omissions of the earlier models and that the economic feedback mechanisms which were not explicitly represented in the early models can be handled without devising new techniques. In view of these findings, the Unit is actively engaged in the development of models intended to gain more insight into the inter-relationships among the separate resource problem areas, and to estimate the likely consequences of delays in anticipatory action in each of the areas.

56. Modelling techniques are useful where they can be employed to obtain answers to specific questions. However, the need for firm data cannot be over-emphasised and there are many important areas where they are lacking; for example, on fertility rates and pollution. Where broad assumptions have to be made, models can be used to indicate the implications of given trends. The studies to date indicate that a general all inclusive world model to answer all questions is not a likely prospect, but that more narrowly based exercises aimed at specific issues can be useful aids to policy making and that efforts should be continued in this field.

## IX Conclusions and implications for the United Kingdom

57. On a global scale the most urgent and important problem is the limitation of population growth. The eventual stable level is very sensitive to delays in achieving stabilisation and a delay of one generation could increase the world's population by 70 per cent. A large reduction in growth rate must be achieved in the developing countries. Experience suggests, however, that fertility regulation programmes become effective only when the expectation of life has risen significantly and living standards have started to rise. Thus, aid is needed first to relieve poverty and raise living standards and to help create a social framework which is conducive to the practice of fertility regulation. It is also needed, furthermore, to provide staff, training supplies and equipment for comprehensive population programmes. More internationally funded research could help to provide a clearer understanding of the motives which influence the voluntary limitation of family size and to find a more suitable means for bringing this about. But in the absence of resources to relieve poverty and combat ignorance, other measures are unlikely to produce an acceptable solution.

58. A steep rise in the world's population for the next two generations is inevitable, due to the current age structure, unless disaster intervenes. This will make severe demands on food supplies. The scope for major increases in world food production lies mainly in increasing the yields of land already farmed through the increased use of fertilisers and improved

irrigation. This intensive farming is of itself unlikely to bring troubles in its wake but there could well be an increased danger of plant disease as strains become more precise genetically. Although pollution dangers could limit the use of certain pesticides, these are unlikely to cause general problems provided their use is carefully controlled. A shortage of either pesticides or fertilisers is much more likely to raise problems; and fertilisers especially are likely to be available only at greatly increased costs, which could well prevent the developing countries from exploiting their physical potential.

59. Although it should be theoretically possible to feed the world's growing population until the turn of the century, the undoubtedly severe problems of providing the capital investment needed both to increase food production to the necessary level and to distribute it have not yet been fully examined. There are also enormous political, social and economic problems involved in increasing food production to these levels. It is probable that market forces would work against the equitable distribution of food due to present income distribution. The resource costs, particularly that of the energy needed to produce the necessary fertilisers and for transport, will be so large that without accelerated economic development the danger is that a major proportion of the world population will not have sufficient real income to buy food at prices which cover the costs of production. To combat this, massive transfers of resources will be necessary and particularly for the poorest group of countries (those with GNP per capita below $200), which includes some of the most populous countries, these transfers will need to be made on very concessional terms. The United Kingdom has recently decided that its future Government to Government aid to such countries will normally be in the form of grants. But the present evidence is that concessional capital flow as a proportion of the GNP of the developed countries as a whole is falling rather than rising. Although many governments in developing countries are now giving higher priority to agricultural development, partly in response to the sombre outlook for food supplies and recent international actions to highlight the importance of agriculture and food production, designing and implementing policies and programmes which achieve both increased production and more equitable distribution are not simple tasks. A firm policy of priority of international aid for rural development and associated food production is being pursued in many fora in order to enable developing countries to make best use of the help available from the more developed areas of the world. Developing countries will also need to improve their own technical and managerial capabilities, and this will involve large programmes of technical assistance from the developed countries. Much more still needs to be done, however, and without concerted help from those countries that can provide the resources, the world's population is unlikely to be adequately fed whatever the theoretical possibilities for increasing food production may be.

60. Despite substantial increases in home agricultural production since 1945, the United Kingdom remains heavily dependent on imported

supplies of food and animal feeding stuffs. Because competition for surplus supplies of food on the world markets will increase as population and requirements grow and because of increasing costs of production in real terms the cost of food imports is likely to rise. There is evidence that, during periods of high inflation, storage of surpluses in one region may be seen as a good investment, rather than a means of relieving shortages in another area. It is therefore important that the United Kingdom should keep under close review the economics of increased domestic food production as the world trade pattern changes and the economics of increasing food storage (which is expensive), both as an insurance against sharp fluctuations in supply and to avoid pre-empting the needs of the developing countries for scarce resources.

61. Other than coal and offshore gas and oil, the United Kingdom has relatively slender material resources and must rely on the export of manufactured goods and the provision of services to pay for food and basic materials. Physical availability of supplies at a world level may not prove a problem, but security of supplies by diversification of sources could become an increasingly important factor. In this situation a major priority is the assessment of the domestic capability in these fields, including the possibilities of recycling, and the determination of the price levels at which exploitation of domestic resources is considered economic. The importance of developing the technology needed to exploit these resources should be stressed in order to create a situation in which domestic sources can be tapped as a matter of urgency should the need arise.

62. The prospects for the United Kingdom in the energy field in the medium term are good, in the absence of major setbacks in the immediate future. Continued research and development of fission reactor systems and the safe disposal of radioactive wastes is needed. Although there are hopes for fusion reactors in the very long term, research is still in the early laboratory stages and there is no experimental fusion reactor working anywhere in the world. However, research on fusion should be maintained on an international basis as a possible long term alternative to nuclear fission.

63. During the next 30 years or so important changes must occur in the established patterns of population growth and of food, trade and energy supplies if world material stability is to be achieved. In many of these areas, particularly in population, lead times are substantial. Thus the consequences of actions taken now or, equally important, inaction will not become manifest for many years, by which time remedial action may well be impossible. Furthermore the effort and expenditure needed to undertake studies with the necessary degree of urgency could well be beyond the resources of any one country. The case for international collaboration is very strong and the United Kingdom should be prepared to play a significant part in such studies.

## X Summary
### I GENERAL
1. An interdepartmental committee has been considering long-term world

trends in population, economic growth, resources and environmental effects, to advise on their relevance for policy. Against a background of public debate on the world future, and a growing awareness of the inter-dependence of nations, the committee has carried out preliminary reviews of the long-term trends in population, the availability of resources, particularly food, and the effects of market pressures and pollution. It has also been concerned to ensure the development of relevant analytical techniques.

2. The main problem foreseen for the United Kingdom both in the short and long term will be obtaining and paying for imported materials; and there will be a need to keep under particular review the economics of in-creasing our domestic food production and food storage capacity. There is also an important requirement to continue assessments of potential domestic supplies of energy and of primary and secondary raw materials. Research and development need to be put in hand and technology de-veloped, so that indigenous resources and alternative energy sources could, if economic, be exploited rapidly. In many areas lead times are long and the consequences of action or inaction now will not become manifest for many years, by which time remedial action will be very difficult and expen-sive. The effort and expenditure to undertake the necessary studies may well be beyond the resources of any one country and there is a strong case for international collaboration in which the United Kingdom should play a significant part.

3. The committee's general conclusions stem from consideration of a number of subject areas, and studies of these are summarised in the follow-ing paragraphs; they are treated in greater detail in the main report to which paragraph references in this summary relate.

II POPULATION (paragraphs 7–15)
4. Speculative projections by the United Nations indicate that for the developed countries as a whole a zero growth rate may be approached by the middle of the next century; in the meantime the population is expected to rise from the present 1·1 billion (thousand million) but may stabilise before reaching 1·5 billion. For the developing countries a medium assumption about declines of fertility from initially high levels suggests an approach to zero population growth rate by the end of the next century and a population increase from the present 2·8 to 10 billion (paragraph 8). If the path of fertility decline were 10 years faster than in the medium assump-tion, the population of the developing countries would stabilise at 8 billion; conversely if it were 10 years slower the total population would be 14 billion (paragraph 9). Though these projections will be revised and up-dated in the light of new evidence, the above figures serve to show the likely orders of magnitude of the growth in world population.

5. On current demographic assumptions, and assuming that the world can be fed adequately, the population of the developing countries is likely to be $4\frac{1}{2}$ to 6 billion by the turn of the century and will ultimately reach a very

minimum of 8 billion. In consequence the population of the developed countries will fall from 30 to 20 per cent of the total by the year 2000 and could ultimately fall to 10 per cent (paragraph 13). Even if the fertility rate were to be reduced to replacement level *now*, population growth would continue for another two generations (paragraph 14). Programmes aimed at reducing birth rates and promoting small family sizes have met with success in some countries. All countries have recognised the right of individuals to determine the number and spacing of their children and to have the information, education and means to do so. Voluntary reductions are primarily dependent on changing social attitudes. The achievement of transition to zero population growth will only be brought about by permanently sustained effort (paragraph 15).

III FOOD (paragraphs 16–26)
6. The main scope for increased food production in the long term lies in the developing countries and, in view of the limit to potentially cultivable land, most of the increase must come from improving yields (paragraphs 17–20). Energy availability is likely to provide the long term limits; but in physical terms the world could meet its needs for the next 30–40 years, and overall protein supplies could be adequate. However, because of economic, social and political problems leading to maldistribution and less than optimal production, even this situation is unlikely to be realised. The necessary capital and expertise is not being provided in the developing countries, and increasing production costs may lead to a slowing down in the increase in food production (paragraph 23). Fisheries will continue to play a significant part locally in providing animal protein and there is scope for development but they are unlikely to supply a large element of the world's food needs (paragraph 24). In the long term, only the improvement and widespread use of contraceptive methods can prevent mass starvation and the resources currently devoted to these problems are inadequate (paragraph 26).

IV MINERAL RESOURCES (paragraphs 27–34)
7. The simplistic approach that known reserves, other than of fossil fuels, will be used up is seriously misleading (paragraph 27). The limits are economic and technological; the materials needed will be available if the cost in capital, labour and energy can be met. Recycling will be important, and substitution by other materials is likely to play a significant part (paragraph 32). Among other things, substitution needs levels of investment in advance that may be considered inherently risky by mining companies (paragraph 30). Absolute shortages are not likely to appear an insuperable difficulty in the next 30 or more years. Nevertheless particular problems will undoubtedly periodically affect the availability to the United Kingdom of certain minerals (paragraph 33).

V ENERGY (paragraphs 35–41)
8. Estimates of world fuel reserves show that there are relatively limited supplies of fossil fuels, but that in the nuclear field, given successful development of the breeder reactor, uranium supplies should last as far

into the future as can be seen. In due course, large scale energy contributions from unconventional sources could also become economic. These and even more so the full scale development of nuclear power will however require massive and costly capital investment which pre-supposes an adequate growth in GNP. The rate of economic growth is in turn one of the chief determining factors in energy consumption. The smoothness with which the world economy adjusts to an increasing scarcity of fuels and higher prices will depend on the early and successful development of new technologies on a scale sufficient to have a significant effect on the world situation (paragraph 39). High energy prices could also have socially detrimental effects, for example by retarding economic progress in the developing countries.

VI POLLUTION (paragraphs 42–48)
9. Global trends in pollution are as yet no more than changes in pollutant levels without proven long-term, global adverse consequences on living 'targets', although further increases may yet have unknown effects (paragraph 42). The need for abatement is recognised and emissions are in general declining, although costs are rising and increasing volumes of solid waste and effluent are being produced (paragraph 44). Radioactive pollution is at present well below internationally agreed levels and, with careful management, need probably not create undue problems as nuclear power generation increases (paragraph 45). Heat from power generation could become a matter of concern, potentially with eventual global climatic effects (paragraph 46). Substitution of technologies and research can be expected to keep pollution levels in balance and increasingly improved and extended monitoring should ensure that pollutants are less frequently allowed to reach danger levels, except as a result of unforeseen developments, accident or social or economic disruption or strife (paragraph 47).

VII ECONOMIC ASPECTS (paragraphs 49–51)
10. The price mechanism will in general achieve the 'maximisation of welfare', subject to satisfactory income distribution, but evidence of exceptions should be pursued to reveal the causes of the market failure. Governments are likely increasingly to be faced with the need to intervene, but each potential case should be considered carefully and it is therefore important for Government to have available as much relevant information as possible. Research is in hand to obtain this and to apply economic analysis and forecasting techniques and thereby contribute to policy decisions.

VIII MODELLING (paragraphs 52–56)
11. Mathematical models will play an increasingly important part in the study of future world trends, particularly in the investigation of the inter-relationships of the subject areas discussed. The broad conclusions of separate more recent modelling studies have tended to converge, especially in pointing up problems of distribution rather than global physical limitations (paragraph 54). An all inclusive world model to answer all questions is an unlikely prospect, but more narrowly based exercises aimed at specific issues can be useful aids to policy making (paragraph 56).

12. Worldwide, by far the most important factor in the future will be the growth in population, occurring overwhelmingly in the developing countries and the consequent problem of providing adequate food. In the absence of famine, war or other disaster a steep rise in the world's population for the next two generations is inevitable and by the end of the next century the figure may well be in excess of 12 billion. Unless current fertility rates can be cut in the immediate future the population of the developing countries alone could in theory rise to 6 billion by 2000 and 15 billion by 2025, but widespread famine with all the political unrest which this would create would almost certainly prevent this in practice. A delay of one generation in achieving a stable population level could increase the world's population by 70 per cent (paragraphs 57–58).

13. Although it should be theoretically possible to feed the world's growing population until the turn of the century, the enormous political, social and economic problems involved make it unlikely that this will be achieved. Market forces will probably work against the equitable distribution of food because of income disparities. Moreover resource costs, particularly that of energy to produce fertilisers and for transport, will be so large that a major proportion of the world population is unlikely to have either the resources to produce sufficient food or the income to buy it at prices which would cover the cost of production (paragraph 59).

14. Unless there are resource transfers on a scale many times greater than at present, the effective check to world population will be the Malthusian trilogy of war, famine and disease. This is an urgent problem, but at present aid and other capital flows are falling as a percentage of GNP of the developed world as a whole and it is by no means clear that those donor countries who can afford to do so would be prepared to provide aid on the terms and scale needed. As lower birth rates seem to result from increasing standards of living, failure to raise real incomes will militate against the success of population control measures and further exacerbate the longer term situation (paragraphs 57–59).

# Appendix I

1. In the Table below, Column I lists the primary fuels, coal, oil, gas and uranium. Generally these are looked at in the light of present recovery practice or uses, but tar sands, etc, are included even though they have been worked only experimentally, since they are among the closest substitutes for crude oil, Similarly two kinds of nuclear systems, i.e. thermal and fast breeder reactors (FBR) using plutonium, are included even though the fast reactor exists only in prototypes. This is primarily to illustrate the enormous difference to the energy value of uranium reserves which the FBR could make, because of its ability to produce and burn plutonium.

2. In Column II, recoverable reserves are divided into two simple categories: 'Proved' and 'Proved and Probable'. Proved reserves are measured and recoverable—a partly physical, partly economic concept, whose quantities can vary with economic circumstances (e.g. the quantities of coal and gas in this category are responsive to the price of oil). Proved and probable recoverable reserves are estimated on a much more uncertain basis and cover all likely recoverable fuels which are indicated or may be reasonably inferred from geological or other data. Such estimates are naturally rather tentative, and will vary over time as more of the earth's surface is subjected to close scrutiny, and as the general economic climate changes. The figure for coal is derived from an estimate of all known and inferred deposits, regardless of current exploitation potential, but economic and geological uncertainties are reflected in the range of commercial recoverability which is quoted at 10–15 per cent.

3. For all fossil fuel reserves, however, there is also the prospect of future discoveries in areas or locations not included in the category proved and probable shown in the Table. For oil, estimates have been made of the ultimately recoverable reserves, which would include hypothetical and speculative estimates, but no recently published comparable figures have been hazarded for coal or gas. For coal there is a long history of exploration which is cheaper than for oil and gas because deposits are only of interest if they are nearer the surface. But there are also areas where no major exploration has yet been carried out, so that ultimately recoverable reserves of coal cannot at present be estimated. For oil ultimately recoverable reserves (excluding what has been produced to date) have been put at around 450,000 million tons of coal equivalent in several estimates published over the last few years (i.e. about 50 per cent higher than proved and probable as shown in the Table). For gas, an estimate in 1967 came to about the same as for oil.

4. The measurement of uranium/thorium reserves is expressed as an economic quantity, although it is based on physical data. The reasons for this are partly a convention adopted by various agencies reporting reserves on whose figures the estimates are based, but there may be a more logical explanation in the continuation of recovery costs stretching to very high levels. Nuclear fuel forms only a small part of the costs of electricity

generation in nuclear power stations, and the economics of nuclear systems, especially of breeder systems, are relatively insensitive to ore costs. However, the recovery of uranium from sea water or from various rock types of low uranium content such as granites, and some shales and phosphates, is so costly that it is not an economic reality for the time being and appropriate technological development would still be needed. For the long term, however, the potential inherent in these high cost sources may offer some ground for reassurance. In order to concentrate attention to readily recoverable quantities, it has become a practice to introduce a cut off and for this exercise the conventional figures of $15/lb and $30/lb are shown. The quantities of uranium are then expressed as equivalent heat content in terms of fossil fuel input to power stations. Two alternatives are shown, one being the use of uranium in the present generation of thermal reactors, the other the equivalent heat content in fast breeder reactors which would provide the next big step forward in nuclear technology, although it has not yet passed through the prototype stage. A comparison of thermal and FBR utilisation of the uranium input is indicative of the immense impact which the FBR could have on the world's future energy prospects.

## SUMMARY OF ESTIMATES OF WORLD FUEL RESERVES AND A THEORETICAL EXAMPLE OF THEIR ENDURANCE

(Excluding some estimates of gas associated with oil discoveries the recoverability of which is too uncertain to be included in the table)

| | II | | III | IV | | |
|---|---|---|---|---|---|---|
| | Recoverable reserves (world) | | World con-sumption in 1972 | Theoretical years of consumption given by proved and probable reserves with an exponential growth rate of consumption from 1972 of: | | |
| | Proved (measured) | Proved and probable (measured, indicated and inferred) | | 0% pa | 2% pa | 4% pa |
| | *Thousand million tonnes Coal equivalent UK basis\** | | | *Theoretical years of endurance†* | | |
| Coal and lignite | 511 | | 3·2 | | | |
| assuming 10/50% recoverability | | 944/4721 | | 295/1475 | 98/173 | 65/114 |
| Oil (crude only) | 166 | 303 | 4·1 | 74 | 46 | 35 |
| Oil (with tar sands and oil shales) | 256 | 393 | | 96 | 54 | 40 |
| Natural gas | 91 | 244 | 1·8 | 136 | 66 | 47 |
| Uranium reserves | | | | | | |
| a) Up to $15/lb | | | | | | |
| Thermal reactors | 53 | 126 | | | | |
| Breeder reactors‡ | 3200 | 7500 | | | | |
| b) Up to $30/lb | | | | | | |
| Thermal reactors | 88 | 196 | | | | |
| Breeder reactors‡ | 7500 | 11666 | | | | |

*Notes*

\* Coal equivalent on United Kingdom basis: 1·7 tons of coal = 1 ton oil and assuming electricity generation for the coal equivalent of uranium reserves.

† The assumption of continued exponential growth of demand is a gross over-simplification. In practice demand would become supply-constrained long before exhaustion of reserves. In the case of oil, for example, even with optimistic discovery rates and a minimal reserves to production ratio, demand would probably become supply-constrained within 25 years.

‡ Plus possibly 1200 thousand million tonnes coal equivalent of thorium, if a reactor with a fuel cycle based on the economic conversion of thorium to uranium is developed.

Printed in England for Her Majesty's Stationery Office by
The Campfield Press, St. Albans

(22107) Dd. 290637 K24 3/76 Gp. 3319